Decluttering Your Life: How to Declutter and Organize Your Home, Your Mind, and Your Life

Decluttering Your Life: How to Declutter and Organize Your Home, Your Mind, and Your Life

The Path to a Clean Home, Clear Mind, and Better Life Using the Japanese Art of Decluttering

Sabrina Godwin

Decluttering Your Life: How to Declutter and Organize Your Home, Your Mind, and Your Life

The Path to a Clean Home, Clear Mind, and Better Life Using the Japanese Art of Decluttering

Published by CAC Publishing LLC

ISBN 978-1-950010-01-1 paperback
ISBN 978-1-950010-00-4 eBook

Table of Contents

This book is dedicated to those that wish to rid themselves of all clutter; both physical and emotional. A clear mind, clean home, and better life await you.

Introduction

Knowing the price of everything but the value of nothing is a fool's errand. It was said as much by Oscar Wilde's Lord Darlington. But that was back then. How does that even remotely apply to today's life?

If anything, I believe strongly and have proven as such on many occasions that it applies today more than ever before when our self-worth is tied to hollow representations. Human beings have evolved extremely well and are in a place that far outstrips what we were just two million years ago.

Think about how you see your own self. The thoughts you have of yourself are very different from your actual reality. For instance, if you were to look at a 10-pound weight, you may think you could lift it. When you try to lift it, you find that it's no problem. Then you look at a 100-pound weight and think that you may or may not be able to lift it. You're bordering on uncertainty at this point. When you look at a 300-pound weight, you know for certain that you can't do it.

Looking at this for a minute from either extreme, you will find the absolutes. You know absolutely what you can and also what you absolutely can't do. It's the border vicinity that is never clear. We don't know whether it is 200 pounds or 201. We will only know when we try. We call that pushing our limits, right? That is knowledge of self. When we start to know how our body responds to certain stimuli, we gain experience and start to know ourselves. The Romans had a powerful saying—"Know thyself."

They also had another related saying—"He who conquers himself conquers all."

What has all this to do with decluttering your life and harvesting the true potential that is innately available to each of us? Well, it is the root of the matter.

When you think about yourself, do you know yourself completely? Do you know that you can lift exactly 201 pounds and no more? Do you know that if event X happens you will react in a predictable way? Of course not. What you know about yourself is not the same as your true self. There is a distinct difference between the "you" that is the subject and the "you" that is the object.

Let's differentiate between the subject and the object. The subject is the observer, and the object is what is being observed. When you look at a rose, you note a few of its characteristics—e.g., color, texture, smell, and features. Those are just data points. If I gave a person data points of an object without introducing it, they wouldn't be able to recognize it or know it. On the other hand, if I showed it to someone and let them experience the different facets of the rose, they will be able to envision it. The point is that the information in one's head is distinct from the thing itself. In other words, there is an object in view of the subject that he or she observes. In the mind of the subject, a virtual object is created so as to intellectually manipulate it. The more you learn about it, the more you make that virtual model robust.

Here is an example. You look at an object that is shaped like an orb. It is translucent and fairly dense. You are told that it is made of glass. If I told you to imagine that orb falling from the top of the Eifel Tower, you would be able to accurately visualize its accelerating fall and the subsequent crash into the pavement below. You would even be able to presume a sound from the crash and the shattering of glass into a million pieces in a million directions.

You can imagine that because you have observed reality, and your mind has a sense of the consequence. In contrast, consider a variant of the same illustration. Now instead of a glass orb let's make it a grapheme ball of the same size. Assuming you are like me and have never picked up anything made of this new-age material, you will have no idea what it is or how it behaves when it interacts with its environment. SO now if I asked you to envision that graphene ball being dropped off the side of the Eifel Tower, what would you envision? Would you see it striking the pavement and bouncing or striking the pavement and shattering? Or would it just go splat like a vat of ice cream?

You may or may not be able to create a vision with your virtual orb model in your mind. If you were a technical person and realize the orb is made of a polymer that has certain energy absorption characteristics, you may envision a brittle object that cracks or shatters, but if you are like me with minimal technical intuition, your imagination just stalls. The model in your mind will not be complete. If you really had to try, you will start making assumptions and base the vision on the assumptions.

The reason this is important to understand at the outset is that you and the thought of you in your head are two different things just like the graphene or glass orb, in reality, is different from the knowledge of the glass orb in your head. What you observe and seem to know is very different from what really exists.

It's like watching your favorite TV program. The vision of the person that appears on the screen is not the same as the real person. It is merely a captured representation of that person.

This brings us to the core matter and subsequent point of this book.

There is a gap between the person you are in your mind and the person who exists in reality. The healthier you are, the smaller the gap. The more narcissistic or egocentric you are, the wider the chasm between the reality of you and the thought of you.

That chasm that exists in who you think you are and who you really are depends on a great many variables—everything from how you were raised to the preponderance of traumatic events in your childhood, genetic disposition, and your surroundings will build that virtual view of yourself in your mind.

We need that virtual self that is in the mind for us to be able to operate effectively within the world around us. We often ask ourselves or others, "Where do you see yourself in ten years?" We instinctively have that vision of our self in our mind, and we imagine an environment that we would like to place our self in at some arbitrary point in the future. Have you done that?

That's what we all do, and for that to work, we need to build that stage in our mind. Can a child in a village deep in the hills of the Himalayas spontaneously imagine that he would like to travel to Mars when he hasn't learned of it? No, because he has not populated the stage in his mind with the concept, the possibility, or the ability to see that someone can go to the planet. He doesn't know that it is possible.

Take, for instance, Sir Roger Banister. He was an Oxford neurologist and the first man to run a mile in under four minutes. Before he did it, scientists were convinced that human physiology could not combine the speed and endurance necessary to run a mile in less than four minutes. For years athletes had tried but failed. The problem was complex back then to juggle speed and distance. Sprinters would run fast but not have the endurance to make it that far. Long distance runners would have the necessary endurance but still couldn't do it. So it was called the four-minute-mile barrier.   It was a certainty that it couldn't be broken. Then Roger Bannister comes along and knocks that prediction off its stand. What was a certain barrier got busted, and what happened next was that more than forty other athletes started to run a mile in under four minutes. It wasn't that we evolved as a species; it was that once we saw that something was possible, we were able to incorporate that in our vision, and that made it possible.

We talk about this in a lot of new age motivation in terms of visualization.

That visualization that we invoke is related to the virtual self we create. What we put on that virtual stage is up to us. As long as we can see it and feel comfortable with it, we tend to move toward it in this physical world.

The virtual world we create in our head is an essential part of living. Without it, we will not be able to interact with the world around us. When we are placed in unfamiliar surroundings, it is unfamiliar because we have no virtual representation of it in our mind's virtual stage.

Look at it this way: if you want a spicy condiment in your dish, your mind refers to hot peppers, and you have an idea of the level of heat that you can expect from a particular spice. The knowledge of that pepper allows you to project what it would taste like and how much you need to add.

As we mature in life, we gain a higher level of accuracy in our virtual world that is constructed in our head. Most of that is held in a subconscious space; others are conscious in their existence. That's why you make a better judgment when faced with a situation. Your virtual construct is highly accurate, and you can make better decisions and face better outcomes. The details of that will be the subject of a different book. For now, the point that we are laboring to construct is a foundation for the concept and structure of decluttering.

On the one hand, there is the physical world and on the other a virtual world, and they both influence each other in different ways. The virtual construct in the mind predicts outcomes, and the real world teaches by example so that the virtual world can learn its surroundings, and that allows it to make better predictions and thereby enjoy better outcomes.

The first time you see a crystal champagne flute fall from your hand, you observe that it shatters when it hits the floor. Your virtual world construct is updated with the new information, and the next time you handle a flute you take care in how you handle it because you know it might fall. Even though we don't envision it, we subconsciously know it. Some people with a heightened fear response, however, can actually envision it falling from their hands, and that tends to make them anxious.

This virtual construct is so important that it is one of the five fears that is hardwired in our neurology. The human brain comes preinstalled with a set of fears that allow us to survive and thrive. It is the basis of fight or flight, and it is also the basis for anxiety and progress.

This represents your ego but not the concept advanced by Freud in his ego, superego, and id definitions. In this book, the ego we are referring to is the view you have of yourself. Ego in itself is not a bad word, but it developed that reputation over time to become synonymous with a person who has an overinflated ego. So when a person is obnoxious, we tend to think of them as someone with an inflated ego or just someone with an ego for short. In reality, we all have egos, and we all have egos that have a gap between what we really are, who we really are, and our potential to really construct what the ego will look like. In some people, there is no difference at all, and we refer to those people as having no ego at all, which may be confusing.

A person who has no inflated ego understands the truth of himself and therefore the nature of all things around him. The image he portrays of himself on his virtual stage is identical to the person he is in reality. A person with an inflated ego has considerable daylight between his physical self and his virtual self.

In some cases, that extra ego may be good because it allows them to visualize what they want to be in the future and may drive some people to strive toward it, but someone who doesn't strive to a picture they have of themselves ends up looking for other ways to validate that virtual picture in their head.

In most cases, the way to do it is to seek praise from others or participate in chain association, which, in practice, is like when you see something (stimuli) and it triggers a memory, which then triggers a different memory, and that memory triggers a random thought, and that, in turn, triggers some kind of physical response or emotion. That is a chain association where it starts with one stimulus, subsequently triggering others in a chain reaction.

Because of this chain association, the human mind eventually finds handles to attach to various items and concepts. These handles and descriptors can be pretty sophisticated. Take, for instance, when you describe someone's character as being "like a rock." You obviously know that the person is not a statue, but you realize they are strong and solid. You attribute all the characteristics of a rock to the person being described by it. That is, in part, possible because of chain association. You associate a number of features with the rock—e.g., strong, silent, hard, and instead of listing all the features or most of them to describe someone, you just say he is like a rock. You just use a single descriptor.

Your mind makes sense of things that are complex by grouping certain features and seeing them as one object. We do this in all things. We do it with racism, bias, and sexism. By associating one object with another, the existing virtual object is easier to understand.

In the same way, we use objects and physical items to associate, or to portray through association, the quantity and quality of our worth. We associate our worth in the expensive items that are available for sale and overlook the refinement of the product. We look at brand names that are expensive and when we can't afford them, resort to fake or imitation goods so that we can feel that hollow sense of accomplishment. But it is not real. Even if we steal the money and buy the authentic designer brand, we are still merely focusing on the associative object but not on its core value.

This is when decluttering applies. There are four levels of decluttering that you should think about. The first is about not wasting resources on things that physically clutter your space and your mind (finance—resource allocation). The second is the time you spend thinking about the object—from the point of acquisition to the maintenance, care, and protection of the object (mental—distraction). Third, you should think about the associative aspect of owning and keeping things (psychological—the void you are really trying to fill). Finally, the metaphysical aspect of decluttering is important so that you remove the associations of one thing with another and start to see things for what they truly are.

As we peel through the chapters of this book, you will start to see how they affect you and how you can go about reducing their effect on your life.

**

Chapter 1: The Complexity of Individuals

The quality of each person is made up of a number of complex factors, including physical aspects, conceptual frameworks, and experiences. There is also the factor of time that allows us to grow and experience new things. This quality of life, which gives us happiness and contentment, does not merely stop at the abundance of air, food, and water but includes another life that has different facets, and they do not merely stop at our relationships and the food, air, and water we have available to us.

We also see ourselves the way others see us. This is a validation of who we are, and it is one of the things that causes us endless grief. That popular saying by a celebrity—"We buy things we don't want with money we don't have to impress people we don't even like"—rings true.

It happens that regardless of who the other person is we value the way they see us and the manner in which they think of us. To elicit that thought, we adorn ourselves with things we can't afford, which should tell us that some things are more important than money, and in this case, it is our self-image. Some people are willing to spend money on things they can't afford to validate themselves through the impression of others.

In other words, our self-worth depends on three things: (1) how we see ourselves without any outside influence, (2) how others see us marked by their comments and feedback (in the social world, it is how many retweets or likes we get), and (3) how we think others see us. This is very different from how others see us, and it is very different from how we see ourselves.

The equation hangs in a delicate balance and gravitates across extremes, resting momentarily in any possible combination of the three. At any one point in time, or in a particular situation, the balance alters and influences our actions and our accumulation of things we don't need and things that clutter our physical space and mind.

This is also the reason behind the confusion of price and value. We associate a higher price with higher value. Once that association is made, we seem to forget that value was the original intention, but we descend to paying a higher price. Eventually, if something is higher priced, we think it gives us better value. Then that progresses and attaches a price to a brand, and that brand then takes the place of price, which earlier took the place of value. Once that brand is associated with value, then a knockoff that looks the same can be substituted, and the person who equates his or her value to the object is now willing to pay a small amount for a knockoff to project a view of accomplishment to the outside world so that the outside world can think better of them.

Why do you own stuff that is not directly related to your living? Decluttering is not about getting rid of everything and living in absolute poverty with just enough to feed you when you are hungry. As the name implies, decluttering is identifying those things in your life that have no utility or purpose to your life that is righteous.

Do you see anything wrong with the picture of accumulating things that have no purpose? If you do, then let's take it one step further. If you don't, maybe this step will give you a different perspective on the matter.

Clutter clouds our minds in terms of how we see ourselves. At the bottom of it all exists a notion that we are unable to survive without these things. We need the appreciation in the form of adulation or admiration of those around us. A movie or reality star needs his or her fan base to adore him or her and will do whatever they think is necessary to project that quality. What that movie star does is no different from what we do in our daily life. The lengths to which we will go to post things that get the most interaction on social media is an indication of the way humans are wires. We need acceptance and admiration to be able to be certain that we are who we imagine we are.

It starts in childhood. We need the acceptance of parents and family, and then we need the acceptance of friends, which is why we instinctively deny someone friendship when we do not like what they have done.

All these fragments start to add up over time until we start to forget what the original purpose of our need for approval and our need for things was in the beginning. Our need for approval is a vestige of our early ancestors who were starting off as a civilization. It leads to conformity. Copying others' styles and looking for what is popular are all shadows of our need to conform and be accepted. It is also part of the five layers of fear.

We could talk all day about the elements of fear, and that will only serve to open up another rabbit hole to meander through, but without getting too deep into it, I feel it is important that we introduce the source of fear that is within all humans. In general, there are five fears that are hardwired in our primal brain in the amygdala and have control over a wide range of homeostatic and subconscious systems. The first fear, which is the primary driver of all things, is the fear of death. Our purpose has always been to survive. Everything that has evolved within us—the ability to adapt and thrive—is based on our purpose to live, and so one fear that drives us is the fear of death. It is the fear of our physical body.

The second is the fear of mutilation. This fear has to do with the cessation of functionality and the pain that it may cause. Having one's limbs severed will alter one's life, and so that is a major fear.

The third is the fear of losing one's freedom. That is the fear of being shut in, incarcerated, or losing one's mobility. We equate cars and vehicles with this kind of freedom, and it is hard to consider living in one's vehicle in an effort to reduce energy consumption, but that is a topic for another day.

The fourth is the fear of abandonment. This fear leads us to do things that will prevent others from leaving us, but this can sometimes be counterproductive. It is left over from the internal desire to form groups and share responsibilities that will allow more to get done.

Finally, there is the fear of losing the ego. Remember that virtual self that we construct in our heads. That is an important part of how we interact with the rest of the world. If we do not have that, our ability to foresee, predict, and plot our course forward will be diminished. It's like the earlier example when we couldn't predict what the ball of unknown material would do when it fell to the floor. We couldn't game anything out, and we wouldn't be able to visualize our efforts.

It is also the reason behind how the art of visualization works and how we visualize we can make things happen in the real world.

With this understanding of fear, as cursory as it may be, we can get under way in our quest to understand the reason behind the clutter that we accumulate. Clutter validates the virtual self—the ego; it satisfies our need to conform and thereby be accepted. That's two out of five fears that we possess, and that is why clutter is such a large part of all we do and why it is so prevalent in so many lives.

But it doesn't have to be this way.

The idea of decluttering burns the problem from both ends. It teaches us that we have worth separate from the value of what we possess and unrelated to it. Think about philosophers and artists. They provide such a deep value to those around them, yet they are some of the poorest people in the world. Does money or possession mark their worth? Of course not. But their contribution is of high value.

When Gandhi set about peaceful resistance to British occupation of his country, he lost everything, but his values remained, and his contribution was without parallel or measure. But he died a poor man. Not only did he make his own clothes, on principle, but he also even made the cloth for those clothes. Did the world think he was any less worthy? No. His funeral procession was witnessed in person by more than a million people that lined the streets and by scores of foreign dignitaries. Albert Einstein is quoted as saying, "Generations to come will scarcely believe that such a one as this ever in flesh and blood walked upon this earth."

Yet he owned nothing, and he relied on nothing.

Much of what we do in terms of this desire to be surrounded by clutter comes from the teaching of our parents. It is then reinforced by our friends and then compounded by media and entertainment. We don't need to stop all these things and reject all of them; instead, we merely need to think for ourselves without jumping to the easily digestible associations. Our self-worth should arise from what we do, not what we possess. That's the first edge of the two-edged blade.

The second edge is that we should find value and make the ego we project in our head less dependent on the clutter that surrounds others in order to define our self-worth and by extension ourselves.

We are debilitated by the constant bombardment of commercials, movies, and styles that penetrate every aspect of our lives. The general public here in America is overweight because we eat junk food. We are in credit card debt up to our eyeballs because we need the knock and the high of purchases to make us feel good about ourselves, and we find an easy way out of things, including illnesses, by overmedicating our symptoms. We do everything we can across the board to assuage the symptoms and the superficial but do not lift a finger to reach the root cause of why we eat junk food or spend so much on clutter or have broken relationships.

All these things happen because we fail to spend some time thinking about all the things that are right.

When we stop to think, what initially seems like a good idea then turns to dust. If you really think about it, why do we have so much clutter? The points in this book are merely a map for you to find your own reasons, but for that to happen, you need to stop and think.

***

Chapter 2: Are you Cluttered?

Before we proceed any further, it would be a disservice to not give a cursory nod to the factors that make one considered to be cluttered or just short of the line. Unlike grades in school, there really isn't a way of placing an arbitrary set of issues and saying that if you have X, Y, and Z then you are cluttered and need to declutter. That is not a good way of doing it.

Instead, use this list as a way to get an idea of how you already feel about your own sense of having clutter in your life. No one can tell you if you don't already suspect it or know it yourself. As such, you are your own first line of defense, and for this to happen, you need to be aware of your own state and state of mind. To help you along and give you the framework to set your objectives, here are the six signs to consider.

1. Anxiety

Whenever we have less than what we are meant to have in our life, we get an unexplained feeling of nervousness and anxiety. While anxiety is a subject for a whole different volume of books, anxiety within this context is related to the subconscious knowledge that there is something amiss but not knowing how to identify it. You know it in a nagging and invisible form, but you will not be able to put your finger on it, and that will cause you to trigger fear centers in your brain that will lead to a general state of anxiety. Someone very dear to me once went thought violent and deeply invasive anxiety that was related to the act of hoarding and clutter. It took close to a year to get this person out of this state, and one of the methods was to rip off the Band-Aid® and get rid of what this person had accumulated.

Anxiety comes in many forms, and the anxiety that you feel when it is accompanied by decluttering is usually aged temporarily with retail therapy or by even taking inventory of the things that you have accumulated. Some people who can't buy things go back and look at what they have purchased and either clean them, dust them off, move them around and display them, or just take them out, wear them for a while, and put them away. Once they do this, their anxiety subsides, and they feel better, further binding them to the things they accumulated. Imagine having to throw away the things you believe make you feel better. It will never happen if you think about it or allow your feelings to do it. The body that you feel to not just the stuff you have but the act of getting more stuff is what is leading to the clutter, and that physical clutter is advancing the emotional and mental clutter in your mind and soul. You need to be free from your stuff and your anxiety. If you can afford it, one of the tricks to hack this system is to go on an extended vacation. You can even find a job in a new city and go there. When you move, just take one bag with you filled with your essentials. You will find that the high you get from travel and the new location will give you respite from the use of the old stuff and an appreciation of the new. You just have to be mindful to stop buying new stuff in the new place. At the very least, it will help with the anxiety. Once you go on vacation, see how much you can live life and even live better without those things you thought were the heart and soul of your existence.

Even when you have anxieties that cannot be subdued by buying stuff or wallowing in the stuff, it doesn't mean that clutter is not the problem. There is still clutter in your head and heart in terms of mental and emotional clutter, and these need to be jettisoned like starships in movies do to junk before they jump to light speed.

If you notice that the anxiety has no place in reality and that all the things that make you anxious, prospectively, never come to pass, then you can assume that your mind is creating the possible events in your head to trigger the visceral discomfort. Your only way out is to get rid of the clutter in your head, and to do that, you need to start with the clutter in your space.

Many people constantly lead cluttered lives, fall ill for no discernable reason, and live mediocre lives. Is this you? Do you get headaches or migraines frequently? Do you fall ill for no apparent reason? Does your doctor tell you that you have a diminished immune system? All these are symptoms of anxiety based on emotional clutter. While the stuff you have in your living room (the physical clutter) is not doing it directly, the emotional clutter in your heart is doing it without a doubt. This a certain sign that you are cluttered.

As you read more about clutter in this book, clutter is not just related to what you have around the house. It is also the strands of thought, emotion, and fragments of experiences that you are not letting go of but are obsessing over and holding onto. It is even related to the ill notions that you harbor of other people's successes over your failures. Even the imagination that causes you fear that you hold onto are things that clutter your life and build the anxiety that manifests in strong and physical ways.

2. Frustration

Frustration and anxiety are different, and one way that you can identify that the time has come for you to start getting rid of the things that have a stranglehold on you is when you have a constant and inexplicable sense of frustration. You know that frustration you have with your spouse or your children—even frustration that may be felt toward your parents and colleagues. Most of the time that frustration, especially when it spreads across all your social circles like a large tarp, is telling you that the problem is not them, and the only common denominator is you. They can't all be wrong or frustrating.

So then it is time to look at your own life and your own causes of frustration. Again, anytime you have words or there is a string of issues between you and your circles and you find that your stuff gives you the best method of reconciliation, you might want to consider that the clutter in you is clouding everything else.

Frustrations are a two-edged blade. There are good frustrations that teach you to grow, and there are bad frustrations that engulf you. When your frustration is the consequence of clutter, it will cause you to implode. When used without making you discontent, frustration can be put to good use, but when it triggers other bad habits and behavior, it is a sign that there is emotional or mental clutter at the root of the matter.

The other way to approach frustration is to look at what should obviously be a nonissue but is never a nonissue for you. You seem to take offense by it, and that is a major cause for your bad days. These are kids of clutter that we tend to refer to as a chip on one's shoulder.

Frustration and anxiety are cousins, but anxiety is more visceral and deep-seated, while frustration is more psychological. In most cases, the path to full-blown problems lead thought one then the other. When you declutter and come out from under the burden of accumulation and acquisition, frustration and anxiety will drastically diminish in the short term and then dissolve completely in the midterm.

3. Desire and Accumulation

Do you have an insatiable desire to buy things? Do you look for reasons to buy new stuff? Do you do a lot of online shopping? Do you like going to the mall even when you have nothing to buy but are willing to window-shop? Do you look at a person based on how much they have or what they have? Do you hope to reflect that person in terms of what you own?

The desire to own things and accumulate stuff is a sign that you have the propensity to be cluttered. It is not always only a sign of susceptibility to advertising and the power of suggestion. It is also an ingrown tendency to see yourself in the things that you buy, and that tendency then evolves.

At the beginning of this book, we talked about the psychology behind this point. One starts by trying to associate the things they see their ego as part of, and then they get into the habit of buying things, and then they get into the habit of accumulating them. Sooner or later, they get into the habit of just accumulating and storing things to feel good about themselves. In their mind, the power of association has made them erroneously think that the person they want to become is somehow fulfilled by what they accumulate.

It is as though the right car or the right clothes will give you a fuller life or a happier one. It is as though if the clothes are a certain brand they make you a better person. Gandhi wore a loincloth that he wove himself at home, yet he marched against the British Empire to gain his country's independence. Not one shot was fired in the pursuit of freedom because the energy this man had was directed toward his real goals, and he had an uncluttered view of everything that was around him.

Buying things does indeed make you happy. It is a measurable happiness that happens at the point of purchase and may last for a few moments, but it ends. The high is lost, and the happiness you were looking for and received has evaporated. The thing that you purchased is still there, and the funds you spent on it are gone. That purchase experience becomes a rush and then a habit. That fuels the desire.

Here is what happens though: after the thrill of the purchase, you long for the next purchase to feel that same thrill. But no matter what happens, you are not going to feel that thrill. When I bought my first car with money out of my own pocket, I felt a thrill that was unparalleled. The car I bought as a high school senior was just junk, and it was the result of saving all the money I could since the time I had my first piggy bank. The thrill was indescribable as was the paltry state of the car. My last car was a luxury coupe. It was brand-new, and you could still smell the leather on the day I sold it. But the thrill of getting that last car—my eighth in my lifetime and the first clunker were perceptibly different. I could never replicate the feeling of the first purchase, and I am certain you can relate. If we do not leave that feeling behind or let it go and choose to feel that brand of bliss, we will fall into the trap that leads us down to the door of desire and the pursuit of its fulfillment.

4. Insatiable Feeling

From an evolutionary perspective, we have the desire to progress to blame for the desire for more. The desire to progress in innovation and to move forward in understanding and knowledge are all earmarks of wanting more, but those are intellectual pursuits that have a powerful result. The feeling of wanting more that is devoid of accomplishment and is instead just the desire for the feeling of bliss or the increase in the number of things without considering their use or quality to satiate the needs of accumulation is unhealthy. The path that results from that leads to the doors of unhappiness and internal chaos.

If you are the kind of person who can't seem to satiate the feeling of desire and keep wanting more, there are two possible reasons why this is happening. You might want to take a look at both and ask yourself the serious questions that will lead you to some answers that neither this book nor I can predict. The idea is to understand the root cause of this insatiability. Are you craving for something else that is a stand-in for something that is missing in your life? You know the saying about guys who buy big or fast cars. It's a form of compensation or rather overcompensation. Is that the cause of your inability

36

to be satisfied, or are you trying to top someone who owns these things? What many people forget to evaluate when they try to understand the root of their unhappiness, lack of peace, or daunting stress is their state of mind. An imbalanced mind, and this is not a psychiatric reference, is one of the major causes of unhappiness, misunderstandings, and the insatiable reliance on clutter.

What you have to do is take control of that by changing the way you integrate and interface with the world around you. The less you use things to associate with happiness and peace, the more you can attain happiness and peace in the world around you. Essentially, you need to get out of your head and get with the world around you. It is you that you need to control, not the world around you.

5. Fear of Loss

Another way to know if you are living a cluttered life is to evaluate your notions and feelings that prevail on most days. Do you fear the loss of the things you have? Do you fear that all your hard work would be for naught if you lose the item? Do you incessantly try to insure everything that you have, or do you get duplicates of everything from shoes to handbags?

This may not be what you consider to be cluttered, but it is one of the sources and effects of a cluttered life. Fear of losing something indicates that you can't live without it. You can. There is nothing that you have around you that you can't live without—work tools notwithstanding. If you were a cobbler, you

37

would need specialized tools for shoe repair, and without them you would not be able to ply your trade. That would indeed be a problem.

Time for a short story. This happened to me about ten years ago. I was sitting in a coffee shop drafting out the sequence for a book I was writing. It was early fall, and I was outside. People were walking everywhere going about their day. It was one of those beautiful summer mornings. I was engrossed in my work, and out of the blind side of my situational awareness, a man popped up and asked if I could spare change. I was a little startled but soon regained my composure.

He was homeless judging from the state of his clothes, but he didn't look unstable or in bad shape. Instead of giving him a quarter, I decided to invite him to join me, and he did.

In our conversation, it became clear to me that he was quite well educated, and that he had lost everything, including his family, because he lost all his belongings during the financial crisis of '08.

The loss that he went through was so devastating to him that he was afraid to do anything now because he thought "What's the point?" He would just lose it all again.

Now this is not the common feeling or common story that I have heard in the past, but it made lots of sense. Many people are so afraid of losing what they have worked for that they don't end up working or striving at all. This is the shadow of a cluttered existence. It is the opposite side of the cluttered spectrum. On one side, you are afraid to lose what clutters your life, and on the other side, you are afraid to acquire anything because you are afraid you will lose it anyway. They are both two side of the same coin.

If you feel that way, you have a cluttered mind as well. You need to free your mind and look at the work you do as a contribution, and you should gain your peace and happiness from there, not from the things you can buy from the wages you get. For this, we come to the next section of this chapter. You need to get a clear picture of what is important to you and not make the things you associate it with to become more important than the thing.

A college mate of mine recently got divorced, and she and I had a long conversation about it. She was from a poor family, but she worked hard and got into a good school on a partial scholarship. Between the scholarship and the student loan, she managed to get through college and was hired by a Fortune 500 company. She met her husband there, and within two years they were married. He lavished her with things she never expected, and she felt touched, at first, by the attention he showered on her. Things went well for twelve years until he left his job to start his own business, which failed. Suddenly, the lifestyle that he had introduced her to came to a halt as did all the presents and gifts he surprised her with.

She divorced him not long after that, and within a year of the divorce she dated and married another man who also lavished her with gifts and tokens. In my conversation with her, it became clear that at some point she had associated the intangible and heartfelt love two people have with each other with the gifts that she received. She truly did love him and truly believed he loved her, and she took those gifts as a token of that love and associated the tangible gifts for his love. When the gifts stopped, she took it as that his love had stopped too. Associating tangible things with intangible feelings is a dangerous endeavor. Be careful what you associate with what, and if you are the kind of person who has the propensity to be cluttered, this is one of the things that will happen to you.

6. Values

That brings us to the last of the six signs of clutter and how it influences your thoughts, motivations, and actions. To be cognizant of the possibility of clutter in your mental, physical, and emotional life, you just need to have one of the signs, not all six. At the same time, though, you may be a little of all six, but it does not mean that you lead a cluttered life. It's complicated, which is why this last sign is an important one that you need to understand so that it will help you with the rest of the evaluation process.

Unlike the other sections, I am not going to list a set of values that will determine and direct you to a consensus on whether you are the kind of person to accumulate clutter or have problems with it. Instead,

I am going to ask that you make that determination yourself.

First, make a list of the things that are important to you. What are the things that drive you? Are they shallow and a cut-and-paste version of someone else's? Or are they something that you have been inculcated with since childhood and have refined over time?

Second, challenge your values with your actions. We often say that we have certain values, but we have zero evidence to prove that those values are something we practice. It doesn't make us a bad person when we claim to have a set of values but don't actually follow through. It just means that we haven't found the opportunity or the confluence of circumstance to make it happen. Nonetheless, we should still list it and then look for the reasons we are waiting for when we will make it happen.

For the values that you haven't made happen, look at your actions and see if you have come close to lining up with your values, or are they just completely incongruent?

The third and final portion of this is that you have to change your values so that you can have the outcomes that are more on the road to long-term gain than short-term bliss. You do know how to do that, you know better, and you just need to put it on paper and look hard at it.

***

Chapter 3: Mental Clutter

Another major area that manifests as a direct consequence of clutter is the stress that infiltrates the psyche and core of a person. This creates missed opportunities in one's career, misunderstandings in one's relationships, and chaos in one's life. It is the definition of a life that knows no peace.

Life is not a bed of roses. If you are under the delusion that life should be easy and that working hard is a choice, you need to think hard. There is a balance in all things, and that includes energy expended to energy gained. That means you have to work to get what you want. That is the basis of life. It is not voided because we are a highly specialized civilization. In the past, each person had to hunt their own food, plant their own crops, and build their own house. It was a direct relationship. Everything you and your family consumed was a direct result of your effort. Do you think they had time to make clutter?

Today, however, we live in a world of specialization. One person specializes in farming, another in carpentry, and both can sell their services for a common token and then use that token to acquire anything they want. What is forgotten, however, is that just because we have stopped making things ourselves and have undertaken specialization does not mean that the work we do is any less valuable. Would you spend part of what you work so hard to do on things that have no real utility?

Essentially, all you need to do to find what constitutes clutter in your life and what this clutter is hindering you from doing can be determined if you just stop to think about it and see things for what they are.

You have to remember that clutter is not just the things that you buy and not use. It's what you experience and not use as well. If something bad happens to you, e.g., you fall down, if you don't even give even a cursory thought of the reason behind the fall, there is a good chance you will fall again.

In most cases, this isn't done because people feel a sense of entitlement. That entitlement regarding life and how everything should just fall into place is something that preoccupies us. When it doesn't happen, we obsess about it and hold onto the travesty or calamity. Not once do we stop and think of how to learn from it and realize that everything happens for a reason. Some people will tell you that the reason is to teach you a lesson, while others will tell you that it is some design to teach you. Whatever may be the case, if you start thinking that things are supposed to be easy and are surprised when they get a little rough, you hang onto the baggage that makes you feel bad, and you're going to be in for a tough time.

What has this to do with clutter? Well, for everything that you keep around you that clutters your life, the same tendencies tend to keep things in your head and cloud your mind.

It works both ways. If you are someone who holds onto issues in your head, it turns out that you are the kind of person who will hold onto stuff—even stuff that you no longer need. What you no longer need just accumulates around you, and in the same way, these things also tend to stay in your conscious mind and haunt you, causing you to trip over them just as you would eventually trip over a messy room filled with things you no longer need.

So if you are someone who accumulates junk, it is also highly likely that you are the kind of person that holds onto junk in your head. If you hold onto junk in your head, you are also likely to hold onto things in the physical world. The question is which one are you? Are you mentally cluttered, or do you horde things in your home?

The solution in most cases is to not necessarily answer this question but to make a decision to stop one, and then one of two things will happen. You will either successfully stop both, or the root cause will present itself where you will determine if you are used to mental or physical clutter. From there you can proceed to remove the clutter that is the source of the problem.

***

Chapter 4: Visceral Awareness

As you saw in the last chapter, if you have mental clutter, you will most likely tend to create physical clutter, and this will go around and around in an iterative and compounding way, each feeding off the other. All the time this spiraling loop is running you have no idea what's going on as you acquire more stuff to keep up with the spiral, and you are getting into a habit of even collecting wrappers and boxes that contained what you bought.

Even at partial intensity, this feedback loop is going to throw you off your game, and whatever drive, ambition, and effort you once had will rapidly erode and vanish. What's worse is that you won't even know it's happening, and you won't realize that one issue is related to the other. You will find that you make excuses and find reasons for your behavior, but none of them will be remotely relevant or accurate. Even if a close friend or a relative tries to pull you out of it, do not be surprised that you will reject it at first and eventually put up a strenuous fight.

One reason this happens is because hoarding and clutter have now become an identity. Once it becomes an element of your identity, you are not going to be able to differentiate it. It will become part of your ego and will inflate your ego all while separating your ego from reality. Anyone saying anything about this will feel like an insult, and you will start to retaliate. In couples, marriages, and families, if this happens to just one of them, the entire family hits the rocks hard.

If you hadn't picked up on the problem and someone advised you to declutter, you would start to have an internal revolt. You can only bring a horse to water, but you can't make it drink. It's worse for those who have altered their identity and their ego—the virtual self mentioned earlier. For them, it is going to trigger one of the five fears, and that would result in a struggle similar to a death struggle.

If you want to really make a change in your life and activate your true potential, you need to jump in with both feet. Only you can make the changes that are necessary. Only you are responsible, and only you have the power. Just because you are reading this book doesn't mean that you have that awareness that something is off. You now need to take it from a cerebral understanding to a visceral awareness that you need to alter your affinity to clutter.

You need to have that visceral awareness that will give you the necessary visceral urgency to embrace the path to change. Unless you make the first move and stay faithful to the path, it will not be something that you can achieve. Altering what is already a part of your ego requires considerable mindful effort and determination. You will undoubtedly come up with all kinds of excuses and reasons to change course and go back to your present ways, but you must not acquiesce, and you must not lose faith in your quest to shake this grip that is insidious and omnipresent in all that you touch and all that you try to do.

***

Chapter 5: Emotional Awareness

Let's look at this from another perspective. Some of you know that you need to make some kind of change. This awareness has come to you by some trigger in the real world. Somehow you have started to see the vicious cycle of chaos and suffering, and whatever potential you felt has vanished, and in its place is only regret and confusion.

For others, they may be one step further along the path to understanding, and they may see that the problem exists in hoarding and clutter, but they have no desire to alter that state. Knowing something intellectually and having the awareness of that matter are two very different things. Until you can viscerally fathom the problem and not just intellectually dabbling in it, no resolute action will follow.

When you allow stress to affect you because of the physical clutter and its mental reflection, the catastrophe that ensues will reach far beyond the limits of your being and your existence. It will overflow and affect all those around you and even those not within your immediate vicinity.

Let's be clear. Your physical clutter—everything that you collect, own for no apparent purpose, accumulate, refuse to discard, and accessories that you think serve an aesthetic purpose—are inextricably linked to the mental clutter in your head. That mental clutter is the thoughts, worries, regrets, insatiable desires, habitual thinking patterns, and negative thoughts that plague you unnecessarily and hold you hostage.

Physical clutter leads to mental clutter, and the more cluttered your mind, the more clutter you begin to accumulate in the physical world, and that creates more mental clutter. This is the negative feedback loop. It's like putting a microphone in front of a speaker.

This negative feedback loop is not limited to your personal life and will soon invade your career path, relationship track, social circles, and every other area of your life you can think of (and even ones you can't).

Somewhere down the line the physical clutter will trigger a stress response that will be indistinguishable from the stress response that is triggered from the mental clutter as well. Inevitably, this will come to a head. All the pent-up frustration and negative energy will erupt, and that is the point when you get enough emotional awareness to do something tangible about the problem. This is typically too late because most people lose their family, career, and life as they knew it before they realize that it needs to change. Even if it doesn't go to that extreme, some of you will be living lives in limbo where you have enough awareness to know something is wrong, and you control your responses to frustration, but you are living a passive/aggressive existence that is toxic in the long run.

Instead of getting that emotional awareness and that visceral urgency that will propel the necessary change, I am offering you a way out right now—within the covers of this book—long before you have to suffer the consequences of an action that you had no idea was coming.

***

Chapter 6: Optimal Age

One of the psychological responses that people in this situation face is that they end up self-sabotaging themselves or sabotaging those around them to get back at those who try to fix the problem. In most cases, this will take a direct toll on your relationships.

In place of building each other to greater heights of mutual respect, better interaction, more compatible psychological compatibility, and eventually better spiritual compatibility, the relationship enters a loop that descends rapidly and painfully.

This is not a straightforward path. It is a descending spiral, and the pain it creates for yourself and for the people around you is horrendous. If you are married with children, the toll on them will be significant but invisible to you. At some point, you need to stop and look at what is going on in your life that is a direct result of the clutter you are hanging onto.

The bond that you create with all those things—that which is cluttering your surroundings and causing your mind to clutter up with thoughts and emotions—has a very real, although imaginary purpose. You think that you can't live without them, but in actual fact that is not true. A patient who had other issues had this tendency to horde everything that came across her life. She lived in a small home that her husband had left her when he passed, and since he knew of her problem, he left the house in a trust that even she could not access. She could live there rent free for as long as she was alive, but she could not sell the house or rent it out or in any way exchange the house for money. She also had a weekly allowance that was administered to her as part of his last will and testament.

If you were to visit her home, you would not find any place to sit. Every part of her home from the floors in the various rooms of the house to the furniture was piled up to the level she could reach with all sorts of things. What was interesting was that the things she had cluttered around her dated back at least half a century. Just as you would be able to date the strata of canyon walls, you could see her state of living by looking at the piles of stuff she had. At the bottom were things that held some monetary value, but these were old. At some point in time, she had some resources to buy what she wanted. There were boxes of garments that dated back to the '50s. Some accessories and shoes went back decades. Above that strata were things that were a little less functional, including ornaments and trinkets, but nothing of significant value. That finally was layered with boxes and wrappers.

She said her reason for doing all this was because each item had some use for her. The house was a total mess, but it was her mind that was worse. She had pent-up guilt for things that were innocuous, and she had negative thoughts of people that were seemingly (in her words) out to get her, and she was just full of hatred for all things. She even found time to hate her husband.

This lady is one of the worst examples I've ever come across. It was fortunate that her husband understood the problem and realized that she was not thinking clearly, so he didn't take it personally but instead took steps to make sure she would be kept safe from herself after he passed.

For most people, they just feel they can't let go of anything because there is the underlying thought that at some point they will come across a situation when they will need the item they discard.

Just like the elderly lady above, the problem is that the propensity to acquire and hoard things that results in the clutter comes about in all situations. She mentioned once that she collects everything because it has value to her, and even things that have no value she thinks could come in handy one day. There was one time she was looking for an old cookie can because someone had brought her a batch of homemade cookies. She was prying open various cans most of which were already filled with cookies that were ages old. She came to the point of giving up and was visibly frustrated when she announced that this was the reason she doesn't throw anything away. A few months ago she accidentally discarded a can, and if she hadn't she said she would be able to store these cookies. Imagine living a life like that.

I am sure this sounds impossible that anything like that could happen to you. Granted that the kind of hoarding and cluttered mind this lady had was fairly extreme, but it is a possibility. While it may seem impossible that you will end up this way, you have to realize that you may already be on that path, but you do have the power to alter that path, and you have to find that and make a willful decision to get on that path and get off the one you are on now.

Everyone has this problem. It is not exclusive. For example, credit card debt and home equity loans are at the highest levels this country has ever seen. The propensity and temptation to purchase create the spark that is needed to go down this path. It all comes back to clutter. It also doesn't matter how old you are. The lady in the example was eighty, but what she had accumulated goes back fifty years. That puts her at around thirty when she started. In fact, it was even a little earlier than that. No particular age groups are more prone to this behavior, and no age group is immune or inoculated against this, but just as there is no age limit to start cluttering, there is also no age prerequisite to start decluttering. You can do it even if you are ninety.

***

Chapter 7: Getting off Your Game

It can be pretty discouraging when you find out that all those problems you had are not as acute or as grand as you thought they would be but instead are related to clutter. Besides the obvious physical clutter, we have also talked about mental clutter, i.e., the harboring of thoughts and experiences past their "use by date." There is also emotional clutter.

Aside from the fact that you are affected adversely, the common thread that distinguishes these things is that they are defined by the fact that they are still in your possession after their expiration date or they were of no use in the first place.

The same goes for emotional clutter. Pining over a past relationship is a great way to go down the path of horning and cluttering your life. If it hasn't resulted in physical and mental clutter yet, it will. If you are someone who is holding onto past relationships, you need to rethink the purpose and wisdom in that line of reasoning.

The human body and the human mind are built and optimized to do one thing at a time, especially when you are consciously thinking of something or working something out. If you are concerned with something else at the same time, your mind is not as sharp as it can be, and whatever you are doing at that point in time will not be optimized.

Here is an example. I play chess every day with a select group of friends from around the world. We have done this since college days, and now that we can play electronically, it has become an important part of our day. We play for an hour each day or one game if the game finishes in less than an hour. Most games take a few days to complete since we never follow blitz or league rules.

Two weeks ago I lost a kitten that we had rescued. (This is not a "clutter" story.) Sixty-seven days after taking him in, feeding him, playing with him, and integrating him into our family, we lost him. My daughter had grown especially close to him, and it was her first kitten. She used to wake up at 5:00 a.m. just so she could feed him before he got too hungry.

My daughter was devastated and was in tears for three days—something that had never happened to her before. It was plain to see that her heart was broken, and that completely threw me off my game— both in chess and in other areas of my life.

As much as I could discipline my mind to compartmentalize and move away from a problem, I found that I was increasingly ineffective at all things. The metric that was the most obvious was my chess game. What I could instinctively comprehend on a daily basis would be invisible to me. I didn't understand why I lost every game I played in those three days, which was rare.

This is the effect of preoccupation on your mind. Even those of us who are experts at compartmentalizing and focusing can be overwhelmed by certain things. For those who are raked by clutter, this feeling is perpetual. It is so prevalent that at some point they forget what focus and mental acuity feel like, and they are not able to apply their mind to most of the things that go on around them. This leads to getting overwhelmed at the slightest spark of complexity.

When your mind is in a constant state of preoccupation, you find that the physical world you are a part of can cause you additional stresses that eventually become the seemingly apparent cause for you to hit the proverbial wall. Add to this the emotional clutter that keeps you thinking of past relationships and past altercations and past hurt and you start to see that the person who is unable to let go is the person who is stretching himself too thin.

All this evolves into worries that are unreasonable and triggers the fear centers because there is one critical aspect of fear that we did not list in the section on fear—that possibly the greatest fear a person can have is fear of the unknown. You have fear of the unknown because any one or more of the five fears that deactivate rational thought could be triggered by what is "hiding" in the unknown. When you disengage your mind from all the world around you and are unable to rationally evaluate your circumstances, those situations become unintelligible to you and thus become the unknown. It is human nature for reasons described earlier that we fear the unknown. This fear grips you in ways you can't imagine unless you are in it, and all the while the fears you have seem real and urgent. You eventually find that the only way to break down that fear for even just a short while is the accumulation of more clutter, which is what the world eloquently calls retail therapy.

Don't be fooled. A person in the throes of depression arising from clutter feels like retail therapy is the best fix, but that's what it is—only a fix. Just like how an opioid addict feels ill when he doesn't have a fix and then feels all good again when he gets his shot, the cluttered mind needs more clutter to assuage the depression. The outcome in both cases is the same, and so is the solution. Don't take on temporary fixes to get over a systemic problem. It will only make it worse.

For those who are engulfed in their dumpster fires, they find that a life without problems is alien and unreal. Life is supposed to have its issues and problems. Otherwise, it's not real, and since life is naturally ridden with problems, the only way to keep up is to accumulate clutter and to hold onto all of it in an attempt to control what has happened to you in the past.

Accordingly, they dismiss any talk of decluttering and reversing out of this mind-set as being pop psychology or ineffective and not worth the effort. But decluttering is proven in science and in psychology. When you combine the fact that the brain is elastic and that this neuroplasticity allows you to alter the way you are, you can make your life whatever you want it to be. If you want to get out of this cluttered life and release your full potential, you can.

The point is that you are in charge, and it is you who can alter your trajectory. Stop bouncing around from one depressive thought to the next or from one set of clutter to the next. Free it all up and move on. Learn to let go.

***

Chapter 8: Freedom

Just like clutter is the physical manifestation of mental and emotional clutter, freedom in the physical realm is also the manifestation of the freedom of the mind. Freedom has been a much misunderstood concept. It seems to mean to many people to be the tool to do anything your mind wishes, including cluttering your life or doing things that will harm you in the short or long term. That is not freedom.

Freedom is the ability to feel peace and connect with the universe to explore this life. Do you think freedom means putting a Glock to your head and pulling the trigger? No, that is not freedom. That is the result of a tormented mind or a troubled soul, and that is anathema to freedom. Your tendency to be cluttered is not the result of freedom. In fact, it is the result of being enslaved to a state of mind and emotion that is trapped. You need to understand freedom and unlock all these shackles.

So let's get started on the road to true freedom. To do this, let us start with a five-step process that will simultaneously declutter your physical, mental, and emotional clutter so that there is no negative feedback loop.

Here is your five-prong plan:

Step 1: Understand your goals

Step 2: Force yourself to observe and compartmentalize

Step 3: Resolve past emotional issues

Step 4: Get rid of everything you have not used in more than a year.

Step 5: Practice some form of activity, e.g., chess, racquetball, anything that is going to occupy your mind in a way that energizes you.

These five steps are worded as generically as possible for a reason. I am trying to cast the widest net possible so that it helps the largest number of you without diminishing the qualitative aspects of the tasks that need to be undertaken and accomplished.

Remember that these five steps are the starting point for you to regain your freedom, and I will review them each in turn so that you can apply them in your unique life. All the issues we have talked about—from the psychological to the historical and the consequential—have built your state of understanding so that you can see your situation in the proper light, and these steps will help put your life back in order.

Let me warn you, however, that these are not magic beans. Just because you can discern them, remember them, and even conceptually understand their intention and practice does by no means mean that you can get yourself out of your predicament. The steps require significant effort and commitment to be able to swing things around. The steps are important but not as important as the way you approach it and the effort you put into reprogramming your mental circuitry.

Understand Your Goals

This is the first step. Look back to a time when you were not constantly stuck in a loop accumulating stuff and holding onto emotions and thoughts. Think back to a time when you were free from these shackles and fears. This will take the most effort or at least seem like it because this would be the first effort of waking up after being in some form of sleep all this time. Just as a child takes a long time to wake up from school and hates it, you, too, are going to feel that the effort is not the best use of your time.

What works well in understanding your goals is to look inside yourself and find out what you would like to accomplish. Each of us has a unique set of factors that make us who we are and also make us uniquely gifted to be able to perform a certain action that makes the world a better place for ourselves.

Look at the goals you had as a child. What is it that you wanted to achieve back then, and when did that change? Are you in your job now just so that you can pay your bills? Where would you like to be? Or are you where you want to be but it is not what you thought it might be? Is it harder than you expected it to be?

Put all that aside and let go of all the reasons you are not where you are supposed to be and just look at the goals. Regardless of the "reality" of it, if you are sixty and want to be an astronaut, that's fine. Right now, just look at the goal that fires you up and understand that goal. Forget about the practicality of accomplishing it. The reason the practicality of it doesn't matter is that goals are an insight into who we are, and it applies here as well.

Observe and Compartmentalize

Observing is not limited to what you are cluttering or what you are thinking. In fact, you are not required to observe any of that. Stop heeding the thoughts that go through your mind at random or memories from past experiences that affect you. Do not pay attention to these thoughts but observe them. When you observe them without taking heed, you will. Thoughts that appear in your mind are not always to be adhered to. If you think of the brain as an organ, you will realize that as long as you are alive all your organs and systems are going to be functional and ongoing. Your kidneys never cease filtration, your heart never stops pumping, and in the same way your brain never stops cogitating. If you let it go and don't corral it, it is going to pick up on whatever makes the most noise, and typically today this noise is made by commerce, marketing, and product placement. We see on television in commercials, at the movies with

69

products embedded in the story, and online click ads that appear in the midst of content we search all the different product messages that tell us what object to purchase in order to feel like the person we want to be. They appeal to that ego (the virtual construct in the mind), and if you have made up that virtual self to be the adventurous Tom Cruise type or the thrill-seeking, save-the-world type, then that BMW is going to play into your virtual stage. But it is what it is—a hunk of metal that is just clutter.

Look at how such movies as *Mission Impossible* place BMW cars and *Transformers* place GM cars. If you are a *Mission Impossible* fan, the only product accessible from the movie is the BMW.

Observe these hooks and all the other thoughts that come into your head, but do not interact with them. I tell those who have intrusive thoughts to treat them like a heavily trafficked, fast-moving freeway. Imagine that you are standing at the side of the road and watching all these vehicles zipping by. Would you go and stand in front of them? No. The same with your thoughts. Let the thoughts zip by you, and in a while they will go by without staying in your memory and cycling repeatedly.

If the thought is not initiated by your conscious self, then don't take part in it. Here is a simple three-step process to fine-tune your observation and compartmentalization skills.

1.   If the thought is random, disregard it.

2.   If you initiate the thought, any random thought that is relevant to the thought you initiate is acceptable to cogitate over.

3.   Observe all thoughts and all stimuli that fall on your senses (e.g., sight, sound, touch), and compartmentalize them into relevant or irrelevant.

Thoughts that are relevant are related to what you bring yourself to think about, and the thoughts that are irrelevant are those that are initiated beyond whatever is healthy for you.

Resolve the Past

There are two kinds of history in your life. The first is that which you can still touch, and the other is the kind of history that is beyond your reach.

You are the sum of your experiences, but between what your experiences are and what you do with them is a layer of interpretation and understanding. No one is born with the full conscious knowledge of the universe and all the things that surround us. We are, however, born with all the knowledge of the universe within us. But we are too distracted to harvest any of it in any meaningful and beneficial way. We only get glimpses of it now and again.

Your experiences are the only way that life teaches you all you need to know to be able to navigate your waters in this world. The nature of things is that you try; if you succeed, you advance; if you fail, you learn from your mistakes. You keep doing this to a higher degree, and you keep increasing your interaction with the universe until you get to the point that you extract wisdom from all that you learn.

Most of the time those with a tortured grasp of the past are those who misunderstand the nature of this world. They see all things, for example, in shades of luck and blessing. There is a common misconception that you do good in life, and good is returned to you. This is a poor location to start from. How well you do is not a measure of what happens to you, and what happens to you is not a measure of your worth.

All your mistakes are not designed to make you have less peace. They're meant to teach you. Peace is not a factor. You have to take the hits life gives you and move on as a more experienced person. If you make an omelet, you can't cry over the cracked eggshell. It's part of the omelet.

Your interpretation of the past includes all the mistakes you have made and all the mistakes that others have made but had a bearing on your life. You have to take it and keep trying.

The way to resolve your past is to remember three things:

1.   Life is all about learning from your mistakes. Once you've learned the lesson, the mistake is no longer relevant to your life, but the lesson is.

2.   Mistakes and consequences are not there to judge you but to teach you, and because that is the essence of life, you are not worthless. Your value is

not diminished by mistakes; instead, it is elevated by lessons it teaches you. Stand up to your past, embrace the value of the experience, and you will find strength.

3.   Finally, learn to forgive yourself and forgive others. Let it all go.

This is just the beginning. It only gets you on the path to understanding your type and extent of your mistakes. Find a way to let it all go. This is where physical acts have a bearing on internal conditions as you will see in the next section.

Get Rid of Your Stuff

The philosopher/theologian St Augustine of Hippo wrote eloquently about forgiveness and much about Eastern and Western Christianity. One of his important points is the definition of a sacrament as being an "outward sign of an inward grace."

Much of what we go through in life is a perfect manifestation of St Augustine's eloquent statement. Our physical acts on the outside are linked to the inward grace that we use to stabilize our psyche and our soul. It brings us peace. Rituals have been known for ages to assuage conditions because the outward act of some measure will influence the way we feel and resonate inside.

In this case, the act of getting rid of all your stuff is something that will be a major action that you can take on the outside that will have an impact on the clutter inside.

You should be aware, though, that you have to do it at a fairly rapid clip. My typical strategy is to get rid of everything like ripping off a Band-Aid. I want you to know that as part of my own personal growth I have ripped the Band-Aid. I have gotten rid of all my possessions—from the cars in the garage to the bed frame in the room. My philosophy was to fit all the things I needed into a knapsack. It weighed less than eighty pounds—my necessary change of clothes, laptop for work, some sleeping gear, and a pot to cook with. Suddenly, my life was free from all forms of hindrances. If you're wondering why I did this, it was because I spent three years practicing minimalism, and that changed the way I see myself, which, in turn, changed the way I interact with the world around me.

When I got rid of everything, there was a visceral urgency that demanded I do it. It was not anyone had taught me or what I had read about. I was in a state where my world was viewed through the distortion of "things" and the influence of possession. It was a different form of decluttering process.

The reasons between yours and mine and between one person and the next would differ, but the effect is the same. While on one hand the massive action of altering your state by ripping it all away will suddenly cause you to see things in a way that is enlightening, on the other hand, you will gain the strength to live without the reliance on clutter.

74

Even my clothes were down to three pairs. I washed them by hand each night—something I had never done before in my life—and while my friends tell me that they have no time to do things like that, what I could never convince them of was that doing all this actually gave me more time, but some caught on a little later.

When you get rid of your stuff, you can see the shift in the way you think, and you begin to see that the accumulation of the trivial stuff is just a waste of time. What's more is that you also start to feel the freedom of not wanting the things that you may deem important. When we got rid of both our vehicles, we no longer had bills to worry about, but we also didn't need insurance to consider, and we were absolutely content reverting to public transportation. Sharing a ride came around at the right time back then, and suddenly we had the convenience of travel at our fingertips without the clutter in our mind and lives.

New Hobby

There is no intention to trivialize this section by calling it a hobby, but the truth of the matter is that when you are in the midst of switching tracks from something that has consumed your mind for a long period, you need a way to do something different so that you can remove whatever preoccupation that you have with your past way of life.

We refer to a new strain of commerce as lifestyle businesses. This is the kind of product that you consume because of the kind of lifestyle that you live. Whether you can abundantly afford or you are in debt to pull it off does not matter. That's the financial aspect of it, but if you need a lifestyle to define who you are, then you have a little problem that needs to be sorted out.

You will be surprised by how much free time you get, and you will surprised by how pure your thoughts can be.

These five steps will introduce you to freedom both in the mind and in your surroundings. It will give you more time to do what you plan on doing, and it will give you the time to clear your mind and understand the most important question of all: "Who am I?"

***

Chapter 9: Make a Commitment

Things that you think you own actually own you. Think about that for a second. If you don't think its true, then you haven't thought about it long enough. If you spend some time looking at how what you acquire clutters your physical space, you will realize that is nothing compared to how clutter takes up other areas of your life as well. Eventually, it owns you and your thoughts without any resistance from you. That is why you have to get rid of all of it.

Look around you. Do you see all the things that you have accumulated in your life? It feels like the clutter needs to be housed, secured, and in some cases insured and protected. In cities where houses are small, there are storage facilities where you can store more stuff than your house can hold.

In the last chapter, as part of the freeing yourself steps, we talked about getting rid of your stuff—all of it. Yes, I know it's a little drastic, but what were you expecting—that you decide to declutter but you keep all your stuff? No, that would be pointless.

But the core of the five points to freedom requires a little more commitment than that. When I say all your things, I don't mean that you go and live on the street naked like Diogenes. There are laws in most jurisdictions against that, so that is out of the question.

Funny story. When Alexander had brutally slaughtered the Thebans, the Athenians begged for mercy, which he granted. As a mark of adulation and submission, notables of Athens and philosophers from around the city flocked to meet Alexander and pay homage. All came except one—a philosopher by the name of Diogenes, who had no regard for Alexander and was the only one who never made his way to visit. Upon hearing of this, Alexander made his way instead to Diogenes and found him sitting naked in the sunlight. Diogenes was a homeless man and an intelligent philosopher. He had no possessions and no political or military power. As Alexander stood towering over him in the midday, he asked Diogenes if he wanted anything, he would make it happen. Diogenes replied that he did want something, and that was for Alexander to get out of the sun so that he could get a proper tan. Alexander obliged and later commented, "If I were not Alexander, I would want to be Diogenes."

It is interesting to hear one of the smartest tacticians and the richest man in the ancient world say something like that. Diogenes was the exact opposite of him in wealth, possessions, and even power, but he was content. Alexander (the person) in all his wisdom understood that, but because he had a role to fulfill for his people, he was not able to take on that life but instead had set out to conquer the known world.

When you own nothing, you become part of everything, and once you taste that omnipresence, it is a powerful propellant for everything you want to achieve.

Let's come back to the way we are going to go about giving up everything. There are six steps in the process of letting go. If you gain a visceral understanding of these steps, you will be able to formulate your own path to achieving the art of living a decluttered life.

These are the six steps you have to install in your psyche and call up when you wake up in the morning and then evaluate how you progressed before you get to sleep at night.

Expectations

The first step is to evaluate your expectations, which are not what you ordinarily think of. These represent a toxic state of mind that derails you and your goals. Expectations are inflexible and do not account for gaps in the virtual construct of the mind and the physical reality outside. When you hatch a plan, you see it in the virtual world, and unless your virtual world and the real world are flawlessly a mirror of each other, you have to know that not all outcomes will be as predicted.

Do not rely on expectations. Instead, give yourself some wiggle room in all things. If you predict or project an outcome and the reality is that it doesn't get to that, do not be upset or affected. Instead, alter your virtual stage and try it again. In the same way, learn to diminish the role of expectations based on inputs and instead learn to do whatever it takes. That's an attitude that will help you with anything. If you set on a goal, a do-whatever-it-takes attitude is one that will keep energizing you to strive for an outcome rather than stop when a task is completed.

Expectations are task driven, when you should actually be driven by outcomes. In committing to a task, focus on the outcome.

The same applies for situations where you make a commitment to alter your clutter. Commit to it by focusing on the outcome, not the expected feeling or liberation.

Ninety-10

Once you place your expectations in perspective, it is time to understand what letting it all go or getting rid of ALL your stuff means. It means that you get rid of everything that you don't use. In most cases, it is based on a ninety-10 formula, which means you get rid of 90% of everything and keep 10%. In my case, I sold everything and kept what I could pack in a bag. I also went backpacking through Asia with the same backpack. Not once on my trip did I miss any of my stuff.

In your case, you should start with a 90-10 rule. The 90-10 number is an arbitrary number, but it is a good place to start. Make a list of everything you own— every single item. Put it on an Excel spreadsheet. Don't bother putting the price you paid for it. Just list them.

Once you have everything you own on the list, use the second column on the spreadsheet to give it a score between 0 and 100. Zero represents items you never use, and 100 is for what you use on a daily basis. Be truthful here.

When that is done, arrange the list using the programs sort function or just do it manually and arrange them so that whatever scored 100 comes on top and whatever scored 0 is way at the bottom, and everything else is arranged by the score. When you get to this point, count how many items you have and determine what is 10% of it. The easiest way is to look at how many lines of items you have. For example, if you have 100 lines, you keep the first ten; if you have 200 lines, keep the first 20.

To be clear, however, this plan is not an attempt to take on a vow of poverty. This has nothing to do with shaving your head and walking barefooted on the road in search of enlightenment.

From this list of items, look carefully at what you have and ask yourself if you can live without any of them. If you can honestly answer that you can get rid of some items, then do this as well. The rest you will leave for another day. Give yourself the opportunity to want to give up the rest at some point in the future. My experience was drastic, and I did it for the purpose of clarity, not for getting over clutter. Inadvertently, though, it had almost the same impact. The way I looked at life changed, and it continues to evolve even now almost fifteen years later.

The process of ejecting all these things from your life shouldn't happen in one night. This process should be an opportunity for you to reflect as you evaluate these objects and see where they really place themselves in your heart, mind, and life. It is a lesson of experience and a journey of discovery into your own psyche. Each of you reading this will have an array of reasons for hoarding what you do—each unique to the item, your history, and your association that you place on the time. Regardless, however, you will come to the same conclusion at the end. None of those things makes you who you are. That should cause you to realize what matters in life and what doesn't.

By the way, just because you have made the step to get this list together and then proceed to get rid of stuff doesn't mean you get to go out and buy something else. No. You will stop all buying for the moment.

Things that Matter

As you make the list, you should realize that it's not about the things. Getting rid of stuff is not really about the stuff. It's about the mind behind the person who acquires and keeps the stuff—you.

That mind is subject to a mind-set that has gotten molded into finding reprieve and solace in the cradle of things that it associates with joy and peace. That is a proposition with a diminishing return. We've talked about this, and you have undoubtedly experienced it. The more you buy, the less boost you get, and to make up for the diminishing return, you end up buying and cluttering more. But the moment you get rid of everything, you are going to feel a sense of peace because one of the things that bogged you down was the fact that you had all those things. Ironic, right? When you make a list and start to place scores of when you last used time, not how much you need or like them, you start to see the evidence of what is really useful and what is not.

The point is that you are trying to decipher a list of things that matter. I guarantee you that you will be able to live on less than the 10% you have whittled down because I know from experience that life is fairly simple, and you can be happy with little and be sad with a lot. The key is to jump in with faith and see how strong you can be.

There are tribes in the African wilderness that still practice today an ancient rite of passage. They send a boy into the woods by himself for three days with nothing more than his spear. The task is to go out into the forest and survive off the land and protect himself. If he comes back in three days, he is a man. Almost all of them last the three days and come home. More importantly, all of them come home with the confidence and strength that they can do anything.

You need to go out into your wilderness and see exactly what you are capable of doing. In life, there is only one thing that matters, and that is you. Everything from the clothes on your back and onward are not necessary to living if you can open your eyes and see what you are really capable of. Once you can do that, there is no other place in the world that you will find a stronger version of yourself.

Be Thorough

Making the list may be easy, but the question is whether or not it is thorough. You must take your time when you make this list because it is more than just a sheet of items you possess. It is an inventory that depicts a story, and it is a map of your mind. While you make the list, the sheet takes on a path that will make your quest to understand your mind-set an easier one. It is a tool, in short, that will help you make sense of your predilection for clutter.

The task of making this list is just as much a practice in introspection as an evening of meditation or reflection. As you itemize your clutter, its sheer volume and utility will make you realize that there is a lot in the storeroom and around the house that makes no sense. One of the things that we saw in that elderly lady's house was fast-food paper bags that held the plastic promotional toys. When I asked her why she still had it, she couldn't recall, but she was

85

hesitant to discard it. So we spent some time talking about it, and in the end the rationale on which she rested all her reasons was that she had purchased all those things while her husband was still alive and that he had in some way touched them. Throwing them away would be akin to throwing him away. That was easy enough to understand even if it was the opposite of letting go.

As we inventoried the other items, some were purchased or given to her after his passing, and when I asked her about that, she had a different reason for keeping those. As we explored further, there were more and more reasons for different things that it became clear that none of them really made sense to an outsider but made total sense to her.

The point is that when you try to be thorough in making your list, you will start to make excuses and grapple for reasons that may make sense to you, but you can't allow it to. You have to get rid of everything that doesn't make the cut.

This feeling of comfort that you get is grounded in two separate matters—the item itself and the number of different items. Have you heard of negative reinforcement? Or its opposite cousin—Pavlov's Dog? Well, Pavlov's dog was an experiment where he experimented with a number of dogs. He would feed them at a certain time, and each time before he fed them he would strike a bell. Once the bell sounded, he would serve the meal. He did this for a number of days. After a few days, the dogs would get ready for their meal as soon as they heard the bell, and what was even more astounding is that they even salivated in preparation for the meal. Salivating is not a conscious effort. You can't control when you salivate and when you don't. It happens in preparation of food. So the point is that the dogs associated, viscerally, the sound of the bell with the impending mealtime.

They attached the sound of the bell to the happy occasion (eating is a happy occasion for a dog). In the same way, you have attached the joy of buying to the item. The item itself may have lost its utility, but the joy you had when you bought it or received it gives you a sense of comfort. You have attached that feeling to his object, and that is now the purpose of the object—to give you a semblance of the feeling you had when you bought it. But that is just a semblance and perhaps a fraction of the original, and so to make up for the erosion, you increase the quantity to get the same effect. Not only do you need the thing to give you assurance, but you also need many things. Soon, they just turn to clutter in your space, head, and heart.

If an item tugs on you, it is an opportunity to understand why and how, but it is not an excuse to keep the item. You cannot hold onto things and expect they are a stand-in for life's experiences. Neither are they a proxy for the things that come into your life and allow you to grow. Even pets that come into your life and move on leave an impact on you, but the object itself has moved on, and you have to let it go. The experience of it is the fertilizer that helps you grow, but if you hold onto that fertilizer, it will turn toxic and have the opposite effect.

Tangible, then Intangible

Once you have reached the 90% mark and all the things on your list are gone, it's time to start thinking of the intangible items. By the way, since you now have less stuff and more space, you may want to consider downsizing your living quarters. If you are living in a rental, maybe you can cut the cost of rent by moving to a smaller apartment. If you purchased your home, maybe you could rent it out and live in a smaller rental. Having a large home and collecting rental income would be enough to pay for a smaller place while the equity of your home increases. It is both a sound financial move and a healthy psychological move.

Aside from that, it is now time to remove the intangible items in your life. Whatever you find to be toxic in your life needs to be axed, and you need to do that as swiftly as you got rid of the physical items. In this case, however, you can use any mathematical number to decide where to draw the line. You just have to remove everything that weighs you down. These include the attitude and perception you have of things. It also includes mental trends and mind-sets, assumptions and biases, expectations and prejudices. You need to remove all these things, and to do that you have to learn the art of forgiving, especially the art of forgiving yourself. The old adage of forgive and forget turns out to be a self-healing strategy more than a passive stance on matters.

Getting rid of the intangible stuff in the wake of the yard sale is not difficult to do; in fact, your newfound freedom and clutter-free surroundings will actually give you the strength and proof you need to know deep down that it is doable and the preferred course of action to take.

When you do one after the other, the former gives you strength to proceed to the latter, and the latter affirms the former, allowing you to push the idea of hoarding further away from your mind and habits. It's a two for two deal that gives you the clarity and fresh perspective that should give you enough escape velocity to leave the gravity of a negatively spiraling existence.

These new perspectives are the shot in the arm that you need to see things fresh and to gain a new perspective of yourself and the world around you. Mind you this won't be easy, and it won't be nearly as quick as disposing of the physical clutter. Removing the mental and emotional clutter takes time, reflection, and meditation. It requires a change of space, mind-set, and a willingness to give it all up.

Don't be Sheep

The one thing that will help you dispose of your tangible clutter is to stop looking at yourself or the things you had in the same way you see others and the things they possess. Celebrities become brand ambassadors for things because they are the vessel that holds a wide array of positive factors. People see Michael Jordan as a legend, and so if he thinks that Nike shoes are good, it must be so. Unintentionally, we see our friends and neighbors as guides to who we want to be at times. Just because they renovated their dining room, we sometimes feel the time has come for us to renovate our dining room, too, or perhaps the kitchen if we don't want it to seem like we are keeping up with the Joneses. That has to stop.

The underlying premise when we follow others is that we think they are on to something we missed, and we need to impress them or at the very least keep up with them so that they do not think less of us. Remember that tendency to spend money we don't have to buy things we don't need to impress people we don't like? That is exactly what we do when we allow someone other than our own cogitations to make the decision on what to do or what to buy. It is the mob mentality that has taken on many forms. We now do that regarding political candidates. Don't let others influence you. This is another negative feedback loop: we let others influence us to buy something, and then we get hooked on the ode of buying, and then we get cluttered. When we get cluttered, we have no time to think, so we have less confidence in ourselves, and we look to others to see what they are doing and then blindly follow them.

Don't follow and don't compare. That's the bottom line. When you do, you end up incorporating the wrong set of needs into your set of circumstances, and that can be frustrating.

When you are uncluttered, you will learn to know what you need and what objectives you are uniquely qualified to do and achieve. If you start looking for careers and tasks based on how much you will make and what you can buy, you will live a miserable life. Trust me, I've been there.

Do what you love to do and you will find that your job becomes a contribution. Do what you have to do to earn money and you will find that it becomes a frustration. When you let go of all your stuff and the influence others have on you, you are on your way to peeling back the mind-set that leads to mental and physical clutter.

By the way, don't discuss this with your friends. You will get sidetracked and dissuaded. Do talk to your spouse whether you think he or she understands you or not, but you should still talk to them, and maybe the two of you can do it together. My spouse and I went through this together, and we became closer during the endeavor. The closeness was not just because of a shared experience but because we had fewer things that formed a barrier in our minds. Don't expect this will happen to you, but I am just sharing some of the effects when I shed my belongings and changed my life to live it with clear eyes and a light soul. Your experience will be different, but it will be positive nonetheless.

***

Chapter 10: Be Rid of All Things Toxic

What do we mean by toxic? In the mind, toxicity is the same as toxicity in the things that we surround ourselves with. It can be things that physically harm us, such as arsenic, and even people who by their very presence and words place us in a dark mood. Too much of this and our life starts to turn toxic from the inside. Even friends and parents who are unrelenting in their criticism can become toxic.

We have talked about toxicity in many forms and labeled them differently throughout this book, but now we shall reserve the adjective form of toxicity to people and friends. We touched upon the factor of friends in the last chapter, but now we will look at these people a little more closely.

When I was in college, a good friend of mine was good friends with another person who had buckets of toxicity in him when he was in my presence. Whenever my buddy and I would be in the student lounge and he showed up, I would politely feign a prior engagement and hurry away.

This person's demeanor always made me feel bad about myself. There was never a moment when he would be around that he wouldn't be bragging about something, showing off about a grade or an accomplishment, or engage in locker room talk about a girl he swore was interested in him. None of these things made me feel good about anything, and it would always ruin my day, so I started staying away. After a few times, it became obvious to my buddy, and he made it a point to ask me. I explained myself in confidence, and I was flabbergasted by his response.

He told me that this person only did that when I was around, and once I left, everything went back to normal. It turns out that my silence intimidated me, and he felt that he had to compensate, and in his effort to do so, he went over the limit of normal conversation.

His toxicity was apparently my own doing. While I am not responsible for how others interpret my actions, and you can't be either, we can only be responsible for our own. We have to protect the well of our mind from toxic sludge that others mindlessly discard.

There will always be someone in your orbit that has a toxic personality that affects you, and it may not just be the kind that I experienced in college. There are different kinds, and they will affect you differently. Here is a short list of toxic personalities you should avoid.

Toxic Personality 1—The Mighty Judge

Stay away from people who like to judge others. Whether they are judging others in your presence or directly judging you to your face, you should consider them toxic. There is nothing you can learn from a person who judges. This is different from someone who listens and offers opinions or a friend who cares and offers direction. These acts are not the same as judging. A person who is judging you is a person who does not understand you and has no room in his heart to empathize with what you are going through and what got you to this point in your life. You stay away from them because you don't have the bandwidth to deal with this kind of toxicity. You don't need to make enemies out of them, but you can politely make yourself scarce around them until you are in a better mental state and emotional condition.

Toxic Personality 2—The Hoarder

This is the last person on earth you need to be around because these are the people who are all about acquisition and accumulation. They are in a place that you want to leave, so hanging onto them is like anchoring yourself to a condition that is hard enough to escape. The hoarder is someone who will make excuses and make accumulation and materialism a trendy thing. It makes it look cool to have lots of things, but it's not. This person is very persuasive and holding onto things, and they will distract you and detract you from your path.

Toxic Personality 3—The Moody

Stay away from people who are always in a bad mood. These people can't cope with life and find that being in a bad mood is a way to cope. If you are around them, that tendency to be moody will translate to you, and the task you are trying to accomplish will be that much harder.

Toxic Personality 4—The Needy

There is a subset of people who have severe psychological burdens that they need constant validation and constant energy from those they cling to. On a normal day when the sun is shining brightly and your world is great, you are more than welcome to pay attention to them if you understand that this is a never-ending black hole of energy-sucking power. When you are in a good place, however, you won't feel it. While you are trying to make sense of your new self in a pre- or post-decluttering phase, this is not the place to be. The energy that you expend in supporting the unsupportable is better served to get yourself out of the physical, mental, and emotional state that you had been in all this while. Focus on yourself first and stay away from anyone who is going to suck the energy out of you.

The point of toxicity is that it drains energy that you have, and that process of draining could be obvious or insidious. You just need to be alert at all times and then put a stop to it.

***

Conclusion

The root of the matter in all things is that you have to know the truth. It is hard to know the truth when your eyes deceive you and your ears betray you. It is worse when your mind is the culprit, but it can be. Your mind can be your single most ardent ally or your greatest foe. Each of us is a Dr. Jekyll and Mr. Hyde in the flesh. The man who knows himself and can control his vagrancies is said to have conquered himself, and it is the greatest thing in the world. Conquering worlds and lands does not even compare with man's ability to conquer himself.

Your ability to take on this challenge and live your life unbound to things and thoughts is one of the greatest things that you will ever do. Without your ability to conquer yourself, nothing else in this world that you desire will ever give you the true happiness that you know you deserve but have yet to experience.

Nothing in your life's encounters will ever come close to the happiness you feel from the peace and freedom in being comfortable in your own skin and being who you are without the need to project things to others using things that are shallow and toxic in the long run.

Decluttering your life is a solitary process, which means that it includes you and your immediate family. They are as vested in this process as you are, and having them on this path will make things more efficient. It will also show you the new space that the decluttering process creates between you and your family.

The strategies and methods in this book are meant to get you started. They are designed to appeal to a wide cross-section of people, but they will not work for everyone. What does work for everyone, however, is that you declutter. How you do it is up to you. The steps here are merely a guide, and the rationale is provided in each step along the path so that you can find a similar step as long as it accomplishes the end goal for you.

Best of luck in your endeavor to declutter and welcome to your new life.

If you enjoyed learning how to declutter and organize your life, I would be forever grateful if you could leave a review. Reviews are the best way to help fellow readers find the books worth reading so make sure to help them out!